I0484795

INVENTORY MANAGEMENT AND DECISION MAKING

:: Author ::

ASHOKKUMAR D. PATEL

(M.COM., SLET)

PUBLISHED BY

Chakravarti Sidhdhharaj Jaysinh International
Publishing House
HQ. At & Po. Chaveli., Ta- Chansma,
Dist- Patan, North Gujarat, India, Asia.
www.iphouseindia.com

First Publication: 17TH FEBRUARY, 2015

Copyright: Author
(c) ASHOKKUMAR D. PATEL

ISBN:- 978-15-08712-50-3

Price: Rs.750/- INDIA
$ 15 OUTSIDE INDIA

PUBLISHED BY

Chakravarti Sidhdhharaj Jaysinh International
Publishing House
HQ. At & Po. Chaveli., Ta- Chansma,
Dist- Patan, North Gujarat, India, Asia.
www.iphouseindia.com

Dedicated to my Parents

Inventory Costs

Inventory procurement, storage and management is associated with huge costs associated with each these functions.

Inventory costs are basically categorized into three headings:

1. Ordering Cost

2. Carrying Cost

3. Shortage or stock out Cost & Cost of Replenishment

    a. Cost of Loss, pilferage, shrinkage and obsolescence etc.

    b. Cost of Logistics

    c. Sales Discounts, Volume discounts and other related costs.

1. Ordering Cost

Cost of procurement and inbound logistics costs form a part of Ordering Cost. Ordering Cost is dependant and varies based on two factors - The cost of ordering excess and the Cost of ordering too less.

Both these factors move in opposite directions to each other. Ordering excess quantity will result in carrying cost of inventory. Where as ordering less will result in increase of replenishment cost and ordering costs.

These two above costs together are called Total Stocking Cost. If you plot the order quantity vs the TSC, you will see the graph declining gradually until a certain point after which with every increase in quantity the TSC will proportionately show an increase.

This functional analysis and cost implications form the basis of determining the Inventory Procurement decision by answering the two basic fundamental questions - How Much to Order and When to Order.

How much to order is determined by arriving at the Economic Order Quantity or EOQ.

2. Carrying Cost

Inventory storage and maintenance involves various types of costs namely:

- Inventory Storage Cost
- Cost of Capital

Inventory carrying involves Inventory storage and management either using in house facilities or external warehouses owned and managed by third party vendors. In both cases, inventory management and process involves extensive use of Building, Material Handling Equipments, IT Software applications and Hardware Equipments coupled managed by Operations and Management Staff resources.

c. **Inventory Storage Cost**

Inventory storage costs typically include Cost of Building Rental and facility maintenance and related costs. Cost of Material Handling Equipments, IT Hardware and applications, including cost of purchase, depreciation or rental or lease as the case may be. Further costs include operational costs, consumables, communication costs and utilities, besides the cost of human resources employed in operations as well as management.

d. **Cost of Capital**

Includes the costs of investments, interest on working capital, taxes on inventory paid, insurance costs and other costs associate with legal liabilities.

The inventory storage costs as well as cost of capital is dependant upon and varies with the decision of the management to manage inventory in house or through outsourced vendors and third party service providers.

Current times, the trend is increasingly in favor of outsourcing the inventory management to third party service provides. For one thing the organizations find that managing inventory operations requires certain core competencies, which may not be inline with their business competencies. They would rather outsource to a supplier who has the required competency than build them in house.

Secondly in case of large-scale warehouse operations, the scale of investments may be too huge in terms of cost of building and material handling equipments etc. Besides the project may span over a longer period of several years, thus blocking capital of the company, which can be utilized into more important areas such as R & D, Expansion etc. than by staying invested into the project.

Inventory Classification - ABC Classification, Advantages & Disadvantages

Inventory is a necessary evil in any organization engaged in production, sale or trading of products. Inventory is held in various forms including Raw Materials, Semi Finished Goods, Finished Goods and Spares.

Every unit of inventory has an economic value and is considered an asset of the organization irrespective of where the inventory is located or in which form it is available. Even scrap has residual economic value attached to it.

Depending upon the nature of business, the inventory holding patterns may vary. While in some cases the inventory may be very high in value, in some other cases inventory may be very high in volumes and number of SKU. Inventory may be help physically at the manufacturing locations or in a third party warehouse location.

Inventory Controllers are engaged in managing Inventory. Inventory management involves several critical areas. Primary focus of inventory controllers is to maintain optimum inventory levels and determine order/replenishment schedules and quantities. They try to balance inventory all the time and maintain optimum levels to avoid excess inventory or lower inventory, which can cause damage to the business.

ABC Classification

Inventory in any organization can run in thousands of part numbers or classifications and millions of part numbers in quantity. Therefore inventory is required to be classified with some logic to be able to manage the same.

In most of the organizations inventory is categorized according to ABC Classification Method, which is based on pareto principle. Here the inventory is classified based on the value of the units. The principle applied here is based on 80/20 principles. Accordingly the classification can be as under:

A Category Items Comprise 20% of SKU & Contribute to 80% of Rs. spend.

B Category Items Comprise 30% of SKU & Contribute to 15% of Rs. spend.

C Category Items Comprise 50% of SKU & Contribute to 5% of Rs. spend.

The above is only an illustration and the actual numbers as well as percentages can vary.

Example: Table of Inventory Listing by Dollar Usage Percentage.

Item	Annual Usage in No. Units	Unit Cost Rs.	Usage in Rupees	Percentage of Total Rupees Usage
1	5,000	1.50	7,500	2.9%
2	1,500	8.00	12,000	4.7%
3	10,000	10.50	105,000	41.2%
4	6,000	2.00	12,000	4.7%
5	7,500	0.50	3,750	1.5%
6	6,000	13.60	81,000	32.0%

7	5,000	0.75	3,750	1.5%
8	4,500	1.25	5,625	2.2%
9	7,000	2.50	17,500	6.9%
10	3,000	2.00	6,000	2.4%
Total			**Rs.254,725**	**100.0%**

Advantages of ABC Classification

- This kind of categorization of inventory helps one manage the entire volume and assign relative priority to the right category. For Example A Class items are the high value items. Hence one is able to monitor the inventory of this category closely to ensure the inventory level is maintained at optimum levels for any excess inventory can have huge adverse impact in terms of overall value.

- **A Category Items:** Helps one identify these stocks as high value items and ensure tight control in terms of process control, physical security as well as audit frequency.

- It helps the managers and inventory planners to maintain accurate records and draw management's attention to the issue on hand to facilitate instant decision-making.

- **B Category Items:** These can be given second priority with lesser frequency of review and less tightly controls with adequate documentation, audit controls in place.

- **C Category Items:** Can be managed with basic and simple records. Inventory quantities can be larger with very few periodic reviews.

Example: Take the case of a Computer Manufacturing Plant; the various items of inventory can be broadly classified as under:

SKU Description	Classification of Inventory	Remarks
Processor Chips	A Class	Kept under High Value Storage/Asset Tracking / Access Control required
Memory Chips	A Class	Kept under High Value Storage/Asset Tracking / Access Control required

Hard Disk / Storage Media	A Class	Kept under High Value Storage/Asset Tracking / Access Control required
Software License	A Class	Kept under High Value Storage/Asset Tracking / Access Control required
Disk Drives	A Class	Normal Storage / Access Control Required
Cabinet / Case	B Class	Normal Procedures
Battery Pack	B Class	Normal Procedures
Monitor	A Class	Normal Storage / Access Control Required
Keyboard	B Class	Normal Procedures
Training Manuals	C Class	Minimal Procedures
Mouse	B Class	Normal Procedures
Stickers	C Class	Minimal Procedures

Screws & Nuts	C Class	Minimal Procedures
Power Cord	C Class	Minimal Procedures
Starter Assembly Pack- Instructions	C Class	Minimal Procedures

Disadvantages

- Inventory Classification does not reflect the frequency of movement of SKU and hence can mislead controllers.

- B & C Categories can often get neglected and pile in huge stocks or susceptible to loss, pilferage, slackness in record control etc.

Finished Goods Inventory Classifications and Terminologies

While inventory classification of raw materials for Inventory Management purposes follows ABC Classification, Finished Goods inventory is classified under additional categories based on various attributes including sales volumes/patterns, functional attributes and operational requirements.

Stock Category depending upon Sales Channels

Finished Goods at the very basic level is manufactured and stocked separately depending upon the Business Units as well as the Sales Channels.

1. A normal standard category common to most of the products is the classification of - Export SKU & Domestic SKU stocks. Along with FG Stocks exists a separate classification of spare parts and accessories under FG Inventory.

2. Many product categories classify inventory based on Sales Channels as under:

   SKUS for Institution Sales

   SKUS for Channel Sale

   SKUS for Direct Delivery

   SKUS for Sales to Govt., Defense and NGO and other projects

   a. The basic product may be the same, but depending upon the classification they may contain additional bundling or kitting items etc.

b. Computer Industry is a classic example, which follows the above classification in FG inventory.

3. Automotive Components and Products are categorized into:

a. **OE Supply SKU** - SKUS, which are manufactured to supply to Original Equipment Manufacturers.

b. **After Market SKU** - SKUS, which are manufactured to supply to Spares Market through Dealer Network.

c. **Exports** - SKUS, which are manufactured for Export out of the Country.

4. FG Stock: Fast Moving, Slow Moving & Non Moving - FG Inventory is often categorized into Fast Moving, Slow Moving and Non Moving stocks indicating their frequency and volume of sales. This categorization is intended to serve the functional purpose of determining the sales performance of categories of Goods.

5. Bought Out Items SKU Category: All the FG goods marketed and sold by an organization need be

manufactured by themselves. They could be sourcing items from other vendors or buying items from overseas markets. Global companies normally have plants spread over all continents and manufacture different categories of products. In such cases a particular countries requirement of certain products may be sourced from overseas factories of the company.

Inventory for such imported and bought out items is maintained under separate bucket to be able to identify them easily. Their valuation and costing and profit margins may be different from those of in house manufactured goods. Further imported Goods would have import duty and tax liabilities, which may be different from that of in house manufactured inventory.

Example: Computers and Desktops are manufactured by Global MNCs like Dell, HP & Lenovo. They have established manufacturing facilities in various countries catering to the local and international markets. Typically they produce few of the SKUS locally and the other products are sourced from overseas facilities. They also buy monitors, keyboard and accessories from OE Suppliers. These are considered bought out items in their inventory 1 listing.

6. Other functional categories of inventory: In warehouses, to facilitate operational processes as well as for ease of identification etc., inventory is categorized into many more classifications including but not limited to:

   a. **Stock on Hold** - Inventory that is frozen/blocked and cannot be released for sale or consumption.

   b. **Scrap & Obsolete** - Materials that are rejected, damaged and not usable or those that have crossed the shelf life and expiry date are categorized under scrap category.

When a particular SKU is no longer salable due to lack of demand and has become obsolete, it gets classified under obsolete stock and continues to be valued in the books of accounts.

Inventory Control - Inventory Audits and Cycle Counts

Any inventory of Raw materials, finished goods as well as Intermediate in process inventory has an economic value and is considered an asset in the books of the company. Accordingly any asset needs to be managed to ensure it is maintained properly and is stored in secure environment to avoid pilferage, loss or thefts etc.

Inventory control assumes significance on account of many factors.

First of all inventory of raw materials as well as finished goods can run in thousands of SKU varieties. Secondly inventory can be in one location or spread over many locations. Thirdly inventory may be with the company or may be under the custody of a third party logistics provider. These factors necessitate inventory maintenance mechanisms to be devised to ensure inventory control.

Inventory control is also required as an operational process requirement. Inventory is has two different dimensions to it. On one level it is physical and involves physical transactions and movement of inventory. While on the other hand, inventory is recognizable by the book stock and the system stocks maintained. This necessitates inventory control mechanism to be implemented to ensure the book stocks and the physical stocks match at all times.

Thirdly the inventory always moves through supply chain and goes through various transactions at various places. The number of transactions and handling that it goes through from the point of origin to the point of destination is numerous. Therefore it becomes essential to control inventory and have visibility through the pipeline including transit inventory.

Inventory control is exercised through inventory audits and cycle counts. An inventory audit essentially comprises of auditing the books stocks and transactions and matching physical stocks with the book stock.

Cycle counts: Cycle count refers to the process of counting inventory items available in physical locations. Depending upon the nature of inventory, number of transactions and the value of items, cycle count can be carried on periodically or perpetually.

1. **Daily Cycle Count:** Normally where the number of SKUs is very high coupled with high n umber of transactions and through put, daily cycle count is initiated, where in a certain percentage of locations or SKUs are counted on daily basis and physical stock is compared with system stock. By the end of the month all of the stocks would have been covered once in cycle count.

   Inventory system throws up a count list based on an analysis of the movements of fast moving SKUs along with other attributes like value etc. In some of the system, inventory controllers can set up the attributes for each cycle count.

2. **Quarterly & Half Yearly Cycle Counts:** End of the sales quarter or end of half yearly sales, finished goods and spare parts are normally covered under inventory audit and a 100% cycle count is carried out.

3. **Wall to Wall Cycle Count:** End of financial year and closing of books entails doing wall to wall cycle count of all stocks lying in all locations and tallying with books of account. This is a mandatory audit

requirement and until stock figures are reconciled, certified by auditors and published, New Year books of accounts cannot be started a fresh.

How the audit process works ?

Except for daily cycle counts, all other cycle counts entail counting hundred percent of all the stocks by stopping all transactions during the counting period. System transactions are also frozen until the count is completed.

Inventory system throws up count list with SKU number, description and location number. The operator goes to the location, checks the SKU, counts the qty available and updates the list, which is then fed into the system. The system reconciles the physical quantity with system quantity and throws up discrepancy report, which is further worked upon to tally and adjust inventory.

Factors Leading to Inventory Inefficiencies

In any company inventory management is one area that the managements always focus on when it comes to improving business efficiencies and cutting costs. An inventory reduction drive always yields results, which are visible and releases cash back into business. Does this mean that inventory management is inefficient? The answer can be a yes and a no.

Inventory management function is dependant upon physical operations involving multiple locations and agencies and processes. The inter dependence upon transactions which are sequential and parallel, renders inventory susceptible to inefficiencies occurring in operations, transactions, and documentation over a period of time.

Another possible factor that can hamper the inventory efficiencies is the system setup that is used to manage the inventory. Quite often one can find that the system setup and process defined in the system is not user friendly and cumbersome. An efficient system should define and guide the physical process as well as documentation process. The system process should in turn be developed based on the business process requirement.

In many cases the operations are made to suit the system setup, which already exists in some basic form and not suited to the particular business process on hand. Poor system setup that does not match with the shop floor warehouse set up renders operations in efficient. It is very common to come across complaints from users with regard to non-availability of features to work around the processes; at times processes are lengthy and cumbersome leading to operational delays. Non availability of different reports and loops and bugs in the system can often push the operations teams to find shortcut methods to by pass the system processes and carry on with the work, resulting in inventory inefficiencies as well as inefficient operations. In cases where a company has outsourced the inventory management to a third party service provider, the inventory management complications increase manifold. You have the company's ERP or inventory system on one hand and the third part service providers inventory management system or warehouse system on the other hand. At any given point of time both have to be reflecting the same inventory accuracy and also match with physical stock available on shop floor, but this is not the case always. In cases where the systems are interfaced too inventory in one system cannot mirror the other and reconciling transactions between the two systems can be cumbersome and time consuming.

Health of the inventory accuracy as well as inventory management can also depend upon the inventory strategy of the company and its outlook.

A few companies treat inventory to be a necessary evil and just about ensure processes are compliant and inventory audits are regularly held. They do not deal with and treat inventory as an important asset that needs to be managed and reviewed to keep it lean and accurate.

Those companies, which are aware of the implications and benefits that a lean inventory management practice can have on their business, strive to build good management practices and keep finding ways to optimize the processes. Any efficiency brought about with change in processes adds to the company's profits. Hence they give attention to and invest in driving inventory management strategy and practices, which are benchmarked against the best in the industry.

Decisions with regard to level of inventory to be carried, who owns and carries the inventory in the supply chain are some of the key decisions that drive efficiencies in inventory management. Besides this technology can also bring about process improvements speeding up the sales and delivery processes and to a certain extent reduces manpower resources and associated costs too.

Inventory management is an ongoing and dynamic process. To keep out the inefficiencies in systems, processes and physical operations, calls for active management participation and continuous improvement in all processes and systems that are involved in inventory management.

Factors affecting Inventory Operations

Inventory management operations are increasingly being outsourced to third party service providers, thereby ensuring that the investments and costs in managing the inventories are reduced. This is a welcome trend provided the companies focus on overseeing and reviewing both inventory management as well as inventory operations periodically to ensure proper controls are maintained and processes followed.

Inventory management entails study of data on

movement of inventory, its demand pattern, supply cycles, sales cycles etc. Active management calls for continuous analysis and management of inventory items to target at lean m inventory Management.

Inventory Management function is carried out by the inventory planners in the company in close co ordination with procurement, supply chain logistics and finance, besides marketing departments.

The efficiencies of inventory management are largely dependent upon the skills and knowledge of the inventory planners, the focus and involvement of management and the management policies coupled with the inventory management system.

However inventory operations management is not under the control of the inventory management team but rests with the third party service providers. In this section of the article we aim to uncover few of the critical areas and action points on the part of operations that can impact the inventory of the company.

1. **Unskilled Labor and Staff:** Inventory operations management is a process-oriented operation. Every

task and action required to be carried out by the operatives will impact the inventory as well as the delivery lead times and other parameters. Therefore knowledge of what one is required to do and the effect of the action should be known to the operatives who are on the shop floor. For Example: If an operative is given a put away task, he should know how and where he should put away the pallet, how to scan the pallet ID and confirm it back to the system. Besides he should also know the impact of not completing any of these actions or doing some thing wrong. The impact his action will have on the system as well as physical inventory should be clear to the operative.

Secondly different inventory items would have to be handled differently. Operatives who are carrying out the task should know why and what is required to be done. They should also know the consequences of not following the process. A pallet might have to be scanned for the pallet id and put away on a floor location, while a carton might have to be opened and scanned for individual boxes inside and put away into a bin. The operatives should be trained on the entire process and understand why and what he is doing.

The WMS systems are quite operational and task intensive. Where the warehouses are being managed on RF based systems, the operatives should be able to manage the RF readers, understand how to access and complete transactions through the RF Guns.

Often it is noticed that when the warehouse operations are being managed by a third party service provider and the principle customer is not present at the location, the quality of staff and operatives is compromised and people are not given adequate training before being allocated their responsibility. Such situations can lead to inventory discrepancies.

2. **In adequate SOP, Training and emphasis on processes compliance:** When a inventory management project kicks off at a third party warehouse location, both the principle customer as well as the third party service provider work on the project and setup basic processes, document them in

Standard Operating Procedures and conduct training as a part of the project management methodology.

However over a period of time, the nature of business requirements changes, resulting in change in the operating processes. These do not get documented in terms of amendments and the SOPs become outdated. Thereafter one finds that the new comers who are introduced on the shop floor are required to learn the processes by working along with others where as no training or SOP document is provided to him for reference. With the result they often have half-baked knowledge of the processes and carry on tasks not knowing why they are doing and what they are required to do.

This situation is very dangerous for the health of the inventory and it shows slackness in the attitude of the third party service provider. Continuation of such a situation will lead to bad housekeeping, inventory mismatches, discrepancies and also affect the service delivery. If left unchecked can lead to theft, pilferage and misuse of inventory.

In any third party owned inventory operations warehouse, the principle client should ensure that periodic review and training is conducted for all staff. Inventory operations should be periodically reviewed and inventory counts and audits carried out regularly.

Operational Challenges in Inventory Management

The latest trend in all industries has been to outsource inventory management functions to Third Party Service providers. Companies outsource both Raw Material Inventory as well as Finished Goods to the Service Provider.

In case of finished goods inventory, depending upon the supply chain design, there may be multiple stocking points at national, regional and state levels. In such an event each of the warehouse a different service provider may manage operations, as one may not be able to find a supplier having operations all over the country.

Therefore the inventory in such a situation will be managed in the Company's system as well as in the Service provider's system. Inventory management and control becomes a critical function especially in such situations where multi locations and multiple service providers are involved.

To ensure Inventory control is maintained across all locations, following critical points if focused upon will help:

1. **Establish and outline Operations Process for Service Providers:** Draw up SOP - Standard Operating procedure detailing warehouse operations process, warehouse inventory system process as well as documentation process.

   Especially in a 3rd Party Service Provider's facility, it is important to have process adherence as well as defined management, authorization and escalation structure for operations failing which inventory operations will not be under control.

2. **Establish inventory visibility at each of the location through MIS Reports:** Draw up list of reports and MIS data for all locations and ensure they are mailed to a central desk in the inventory team for daily review. The inventory team leader should analyze daily reports of all locations and highlight any non-

conformity and resolve them as well as update the management.

3. Initiate Daily Stock count procedure to be carried out at all of the locations and reported back to the inventory desk.

   Daily stock count should be able to reflect location accuracy, stock accuracy as well as transaction summary for the day.

4. Monthly audits and inventory count should be implemented at all locations without fail and insist on one hundred percent adherence.

5. Quarterly inventory - wall-to-wall count or half yearly and annual wall-to-wall count should be implemented depending upon the volume of transactions as well as value of transactions at each location.

6. Central Inventory team to be responsible for ensuring review of all reports and controlling inventories at all locations.

7. Inventory reconciliation - involves reconciling physical inventory at site with the system inventory at

3PL Site and then reconciling 3PL System stocks with company's system stock.

8. Visiting major sites and being present during physical stock audits on quarterly or half yearly basis is very important.

9. Lastly keep reviewing processes and ensure training and re training is carried out regularly and at all times at site so that a process oriented culture is imbibed and all operating staff understand the importance of maintaining processes as well as inventory health.

Inventory is nothing but money to the company. If 3PL vendor is managing the inventory, needless to say you should have your processes in place to be able to control and maintain inventory health.

Inventory Health - Important factors to be considered to avoid Inventory Mismatch

Any inventory of raw materials or finished goods runs into thousands of SKU items. Especially in case of Raw Material Inventory as well as Spare Parts Inventory these numbers could be much higher when compared to Finished Goods. Even in Finished Goods some products like clothes, grocery etc could run into thousands of SKUs across the entire range.

Every unit of Inventory has an economic value in the books of the company. Therefore as an asset one needs to have a control over the inventory and ensure that the books stock matches with the physical stock. By book stock essentially we mean system stock.

Inventory management on one hand consists of managing the inventory transactions and data in the system and on the other it involves physical processes on the ground. Both these have to work in tandem to ensure that all transactions are closed and completed both in the system as well as on the shop floor.

In a warehouse a typical day operations begin with receiving materials from different vendors, which are unloaded, counted and updated in the system. The system then issues a GRN and directs the location to which the material should be stored. Accordingly the material is then moved to the storage location and a confirmation back in the system closes the entire transaction. At the same time, parallel processes for shipment delivery will be under process where the system releases pick orders on the warehouse. Operations staff picks up the materials as per pick list and confirm back to the system, which then releases a packing order and an invoice for shipment. Amidst these multiple transactions there would be quite a few operational transactions like bin to bin transfers, kitting etc which are again transacted in the system followed by physical process and re confirmation to the system.

In such situation where multiple transactions both in system as well as physical operations are going on and the tasks are interdependent, any process deviation in any one of the transactions is bound to occur resulting in differences between system transactions and physical inventory.

Current trend in the industries is to outsource the warehousing operations to third party service providers, in which case the transactions increase manifold because of the introduction of additional system at the warehouse end, which belongs to the third party vendor. The principle customer maintains his inventory in his ERP, which transacts with the third party vendors WMS - Warehouse Management System and the Physical transactions on the shop floor, which have to run concurrently with the system.

1. Systems Issues

Normally the ERP system and the WMS are interfaced using standard interfaces. Both systems exchange standard interface files updating the transactions carried out in each of the systems and are downloaded at both the ends in periodic batch frequencies of half hour or one hour. Thus all receipts received physically at the warehouse in one hour get updated in warehouse WMS which then sends out the GRN information to Client's ERP for updating. Client's ERP similarly processes the orders based on the inventory available in its system and issues sales orders which are sent across to WMS. WMS then generates pick waves which when confirmed lead to releasing of packing list and invoice. These transactions are again completed physically and WMS is updated. WMS further sends out the information of dispatch to ERP for further updation. For these transactions to happen smoothly both ERP as well as WMS should match perfectly in terms of inventory and transaction information.

When in case of day-to-day operations, hundreds of transactions are being processes at both the ends concurrently; the system updates may not happen on real time basis and can lead to inventory discrepancies. Therefore it becomes necessary to have daily reconciliation of all transactions between both systems as well as operations.

2. System discipline required

Such transaction based systems call for strict discipline on the part of system users to ensure they complete all processes without deviation and regularly update the masters and reconcile on daily basis. Any lack of discipline can effect not only the inventory but effect transactions as well. For Example, if for any reason a particular SKU or consignment is blocked at the warehouse and is not to be dispatched, the inventory block should not only happen in WMS which controls floor operations but in ERP also. Otherwise in the ERP the blocked inventory may be showing as open inventory and get allocated for a sales order.

3. Master Data Up-dation is a MUSTM

SKU code numbers in any inventory are subject to frequent changes. You can also have the same description and same item being supplied by different vendors. Every time a new SKU is created at the Customer's ERP, one must ensure that the same new SKUs are created in the WMS too. WMS master data with regard to SKU Code, description and other SKU Master Data and Vendor Master information should mirror that of the ERP. If by oversight or careless ness this co-ordination is found lacking the inventory gets mixed up or does not get uploaded into the system.

4. System Inventory should match with Physical Inventory

The inventory that is setup and maintained in the ERP as well as WMS should correspond to the inventory on the shop floor. For example the inventory shown in

ERP and WMS with details of each location as to where, how much is stored in which location should match exactly with the physical reality. On the shop floor the physical location should have the same SKU, Exact quantity as per System entry. Any mismatch on the floor location resulting out of mistake from the operations staff of keeping inventory in wrong location will create havoc in both system as well as operations.

Company's approach to Inventory Health

Inventory means an item of value and asset in the books of the Company. This is the most important category of item that needs to be focused upon by the management for in its management lies the business efficiency as well as profits.

Inventory holding is a must for any business organization that is into manufacturing and selling or trading of products. Technically inventory is holding stock of raw materials or finished goods for a future point of consumption. This in fact blocks the working capital employed by the company.

In any business, it is essential to have optimum inventory at all times. Over inventory stocking results in erosion of profits and increase in inventory carrying costs that effects the operational costs of the company, while shortage of inventory can lead to loss of business and sales opportunity which will not only result in revenue loss but damage company's reputation and reliability in the market and with customer.

Inventory by nature is operations intensive. With the number of items running into thousands, coupled with the number of transactions that are involved in managing inventory operations on daily basis, it is quite possible that without water tight controls over processes, systems and operations, inventory will go out of control resulting in pilferage, loss due to damage, mis-management, theft or shrinking. Incase of inventories having extra sensitive characteristics involving perish ability, shelf life or temperature control, tilt meters etc, it becomes necessary to keep a tighter watch and control over such inventories and their management.

Inventory Control and effective management is essentially based mainly on two prime factors, which are Company's Inventory Management Strategy and Policy as well as Management's focus on Inventory Operation Management. A company which identifies supply chain and inventory policy to be the enabler that will help the company gain an edge over competition in the market and use it to leverage its position will invest into engineering efficient supply chain models and inventory management practices to meet its business goals. Companies like HP, IBM, DELL, Wall Mart, Xerox, Procter and Gamble and Unilever etc have invested continually into reviewing and re engineering their inventory as well as supply chain strategies to meet with emerging market situations. All these companies have done away with traditional concepts of storage and inventory management and adapted the more efficient VMI-Vendor Managed Inventory, JIT - Just In Time and Customer Response systems whereby they have management to get their suppliers to hold inventories for them right next to their manufacturing sites and supply on Just In Time Basis. Retailing business being highly competitive most of the companies have invested heavily into soft wares and systems to be able to manage the inventory visibility and stocks as well as call offs thereby bringing efficiencies into inventory management operations. Systems driven catalogue management, system based forecasting, Statistical analysis of Sales Data and extrapolation using complex systems enabled forecasting methods and reports have brought in lean Inventory management concepts in these companies and their strategies have paid off very well. In effect their strategic focus and approach to inventory and logistics planning have been the key factors behind their success in the markets.

While the companies focus on strategic decision making, planning and defining of Inventory rules and methodologies relevant to their business operations, it is important to realize that the effectiveness is dependant upon the ground operations. Especially in case of Inventories which are stored at multi locations and handled by third party service providers, it is becomes that much more difficult to manage the inventory operations.

Therefore as principle owners of inventory, the companies should build very strong management focus to define processes, set up expectations, gather MIS data, analyze and control through checks and balances. This will involve setting up of very strong inventory and logistics team with right management and operational process capability and experience coupled with strong systems deployment. Companies would have to set up independent audit teams too to audit the inventory books, systems as well as processes both from operational as well as statutory compliance point of view.

It is not enough for companies to focus on monitoring the operations of the third party services, but focus should also be on internal management of inventory planning and operations too. Systems deployed should be capable of generating MIS reports and other data as per requirement. Secondly inventory analysis and review should be a periodic process as laid down by process document and manual, involving inventory planning, logistics, procurement as well as finance teams. It is only when decisions and review of inventories are done in line with changes in demand pattern or other operational conditions coupled with speedy decisions to scrap or dispose of unused, unwanted and non moving inventory will help in maintaining inventory balance and efficiency.

The company should have clearly defined metrics to measure and define inventory health as well as inventory operations health and this needs to be viewed by the senior management periodically with operating management and the rest of the team.

Inventory Turnover as Indicator of Health of Inventory and Business

Inventory management as well as Supply chain operations are often overlapping and hold the key to the success of sales operations. In all of the businesses be in automobile, manufacturing, pharma or retail industry, status of inventory reflects the health of the business.

Inventory operations have two key elements namely Inventory System and Physical operations. Today inventory systems have replaced the book keeping and financial accounting that was being practiced earlier. Current inventory systems not only do the book keeping but are linked to upstream as well as down stream activities including procurement, sales processing, financial accounting.

In terms of measuring a sales performance in relation to Inventory, we often use the term Inventory Turnover. Inventory turnover simply refers to the number of times the inventory is sold or used in a period of one year. Inventory turnover is also termed as stock turn, or stock turnover.

Inventory Turnover is calculated by taking the Total Cost of Goods Sold, divided by Average Inventory.

Adding together Beginning inventory and ending inventory and dividing the figure by 2 in turn calculate average Inventory.

The inventory turnover as a measure of health of sales and business is used extensively in Retail, textile as well as FMCG segments. A higher inventory turnover does indicate a healthy trend of increased sales and indicates the need to maintain adequate inventory levels to avoid stock outs. In adequate stocks can result in loss of business opportunities and is something that the management needs to keep watching closely. On the other hand a lower inventory turnover shows that either the sales of the said inventory is slowing down or that the unused inventory is building up clogging the system somewhere. A slow inventory turn can help the inventory manager focus on finding non-moving, obsolete and slow moving inventory items and thereby steps can be taken to deal with them appropriately.

Inventory turnover also reflects the holding cost that is incurred in managing inventory. Increased inventory turns reduce the holding costs. The costs especially fixed costs like rent and cost of operations get distributed over higher inventory throughput and thereby the cost of inventory transactions reduces.

Inventory turnover is also indicative of the health of inventory operations. When the inventory turnover is higher, the inventory operations efficiency will also be high to meet with the increased operational requirements thereby good house keeping and increased responsiveness to market requirements.

Inventory turn in some cases or some systems is also calculated based on the numbers sold rather than the average value of inventory. In such a system the Inventory turn is calculated by dividing the Number of Units Sold divided by the Average number of Units inventory held in a given period of time.

Over a number of years, each industry has developed methods to check inventory turnover and industry standards have been standardized. So whenever a new business venture is set up, they are able to have the industry standard as benchmark to be achieved and use it as a guide to streamline operations.

Why Young Managers should know about Inventory Operations

When a management student passes out from college and is absorbed into any business organization, if he is lucky he will get to spend a few months in getting orientation in all departments before being assigned to a particular department or function at the end of the induction program. Those who get to be assigned to working in Supply chain or inventory operations of the company are likely to learn very important lessons that is likely to give them an edge later on when they grow in ranks and take up higher and different responsibilities. Inventory management and supply chain operations both on the Raw material as well as Finished Goods side are very critical to the success of sales and marketing besides being major contributors to the profitability of the company.

Sales and Marketing can be said to be efficient not when they build sales leads and convert them. But the efficiency of being able to reach the right Finished Product to the Right Customer or Market and the Right Time is what determines the Success of S & M. Inventory is the other function that is critical to the Sales.

An efficient inventory management will mean carrying balanced inventory and functioning at optimum efficiency as well as ensuring control over inventory carrying costs. Any increase in efficiency of inventory holding or operations impacts bottom line directly. Supply chain, having to do with movement of inventory to and from plant to the markets, holding inventory en route at various points and managing overall inventory logistics is also very critical both to inventory management as well as the Sales Function.

Once the trainee has understood the operations models and seen how the entire chain of functions involving multiple internal departments, systems, documentation as well as external vendors, third party service providers and the governmental organization all work in tandem to make the business a success, he would have pretty much understood the secret to building successful business.

Time and again we have seen that the General Managers as well as the Marketing Managers who have been heading their departments in the companies have made headway and achieved breakthroughs in terms of marketing their products using innovative supply chain distribution strategies and thereby have been able to impact the bottom lines substantially. Direct marketing, E marketing, Network marketing are all new sales concepts but if you have to incorporate these into your marketing plan, then it becomes necessary first for you to be able to understand and define the supply chain and inventory strategy to service these delivery channels.

An inventory strategy can be designed on paper but then to be able make it operational, one needs to have a realistic exposure and experience to the field operations and have a hang of how things work on the ground. Inventory management and operations involve multiple agencies and service providers combined with multiple systems that need to be interfaced. Sales process has to be married to Supply Chain and logistics process, which in turn needs to drive the inventory operations process in the back end. All these different modules need to be working in tandem and seamlessly to deliver products across markets in time.

Any aspiring manager who wants to head an organization as General Management or Marketing Manger would have to first get first hand experience of these brass tacks that will help him later to be able to devise practical and achievable strategies to take his business ahead.

Inventory Planning - Basic Concepts

Every organization that is engaged in production, sale or trading of Products holds inventory in one or the other form. While production and manufacturing organizations hold raw material inventories, finished goods and spare parts inventories, trading companies might hold only finished goods inventories depending upon the business model.

When in case of raw material inventory management function is essentially dealing with two major functions. First function deals with inventory planning and the second being inventory tracking. As inventory planners, their main job consists in analyzing demand and deciding when to order and how much to order new inventories. Traditional inventory management approach consists of two models namely:

- EOQ - Economic Order Quantity
- Continuous Ordering
- Periodic Ordering

  <=""

1. **EOQ:** Economic Order Quantity method determines the optimal order quantity that will minimize the total

inventory cost. EOQ is a basic model and further models developed based on this model include production Quantity Model and Quantity Discount Model.

2. **Continuous Order Model:** works on fixed order quantity basis where a trigger for fixed quantity replenishment is released whenever the inventory level reaches predetermined safety level and triggers re ordering.

3. **Periodic System Model:** This model works on the basis of placing order after a fixed period of time.

EOQ Model

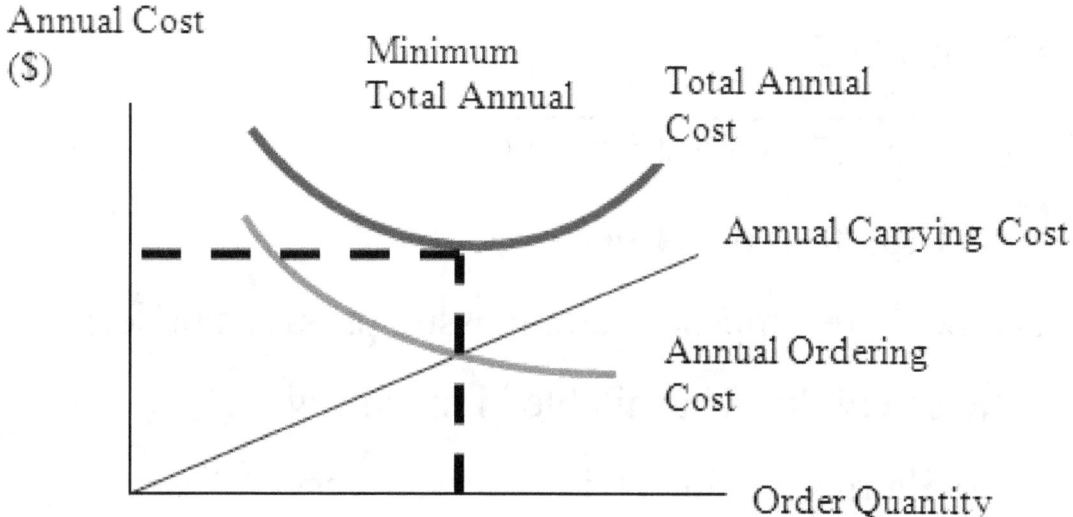

Example: Biotech.Co produces chemicals to sell to wholesalers. One of the raw material it buys is sodium nitrate which is purchased at the rate of Rs.22.50 per ton. Biotech's forecasts show a estimated requirement of 5,75,000 tons of sodium nitrate for the coming year. The annual total carrying cost for this material is 40% of acquisition cost and the ordering cost is Rs.595. What is the Most Economical Order Quantity ?

$$EOQ = \sqrt{2DS/C}$$

D	=	Annual	Demand
C	=	Carrying	Cost

S = Ordering Cost

D	=	5,75,000	tons
C	=0.40(22.50)	=	Rs.9.00/Ton/Year

S = Rs.595/Order

$$EOQ = \sqrt{2(5,750,000)(595)/9.00}$$

= 27,573.135 tons per Order.

This model pre supposes certain assumptions as under:

- No safety Stocks available in inventory.
- No Shortages allowed in order delivery.
- Demand is at uniform rate and does not fluctuate
- Lead Time for order delivery is constant
- One order = One delivery no shortages allowed.

- This model does not take into account other costs of inventory such as stock out cost, acquisition cost etc to calculate EOQ.

In this model, the demand increases for production the inventory gets depleted. When the inventory drops to a critical point the re order process gets triggered. New order is always place for fixed quantities. On receipt of the delivery against the order the inventory level goes up.

Using this model, further data extrapolation is possible to determine other factors like how many orders are to be placed in a year and what is the time lapse between orders etc.

EOQ For Production Lot:

This model is also used to determine the order size and the production lot for an item to be produced at one stage of production and stored as work in progress inventory to be supplied to the next state of production or to the customer.

Good Inventory Management Practices

Good inventory Management practices in the company help by adding value in terms of having control over and maintaining lean inventory. Inventory should not be too much or too less. Both the situations are bad for the company. However often we see that inventory is not focused upon by the management and hence lot of inefficiencies build up over a period of time without the knowledge of the management. It is only when we start a cost reduction drive that the inventory goof ups and skeletons come out of the cupboard and results in revamping the entire operations.

However those companies, which have always focused on inventory as a principle function and recognized that the inventory effects their sales, as well as the books of accounts and profits, have managed to introduce and improve inventory management processes. Many business models work on lean inventory principle or JIT inventory along with other models like VMI etc. Inventory management to a large extent is dependant upon the supply chain efficiency as well as operations.

Inventory management is a management cum operations function. It requires operational processes to be followed and maintained on the floor and in inventory management systems. Coupled with operations, it entails continuous study; analysis and decision making to control and manage inventory levels.

We have covered below briefly few of the points which when followed, can go a long way in ensuring that the inventory is lean and clean.

1. Review Inventory periodically and revise stocking patterns and norms

Inventory is dependant upon the demand as well as the supply chain delivery time. Often companies follow one stocking policy for all items. For example, all A, B & C categories may be stocking inventory of 15 days, which may not be the right thing that is required. While some items may have a longer lead-time thus affecting the inventory holding, the demand pattern and the hit frequency in terms of past data may show up differently for each of the inventory items. Therefore one standard norm does not suit all and can lead to over stocking of inventory as well as in efficiencies in the system.

2. Get into detailed inventory planning - One size does not fit all

Understand the inventory types and the specific characteristics of the items you are carrying. Then build the inventory stocking parameters taking into account the unique characteristics of the particular inventory.

From amongst your inventory list, you will find that all types of materials are not of the same value. Some might be very expensive and need to be carried in stock for a longer period, while another item might have a shorter lead-time and may be fast moving. Quite a few items often have shelf life and hence require separate norms and focus to manage such items.

Getting into the detailed understanding will help you identify the inventory-stocking norm required to manage these characteristics to ensure optimum efficiency. The solution quite often may not be to carry stocks, rather it may involve setting up the customer service standard for such items and specifying a delivery time depending upon the frequency of demand. Quite a few items often have shelf life and hence require separate norms and focus to manage such items.

3. **Study demand pattern, movement patterns and cycles to build suitable inventory norms for different categories of inventory**

Companies which are into retail segments and dealing with huge inventories in terms of number of parts as well as value will necessarily need to ensure they practice review of inventory list and clean up operations on ongoing basis.

Popularly known as catalogue management, inventory norms review should be carried out based on detailed study of the sales data, demand pattern, sales cycles etc. Understanding of the business and sales cycles specific to the product category helps one manage inventories better. For example, in case of retail garments, with every season certain skus become redundant no matter how their demand was in the previous months. This helps identify those stocks which are required to be managed at a micro level and identify the high value and fast moving items that need to be always on the radar to avoid stock outs.

It does not help for example to carry standard stocks of all items including low value items as well as high value items. If the low value items are locally available and the lead-time is less, one can cut down on the inventory and change the buying pattern. Similarly high value items too can be managed by cutting down the delivery lead times and in turn reducing inventory.

It helps to periodically study the past data and extrapolate the same to identify slow moving and obsolete items. The dead stocks should be flushed out and active catalogue items should be made available.

Inventory Management Systems

Modern day inventory is managed by sophisticated system applications that are designed to manage complex inventory plans and to a large extent contain processes that initiate and streamline the operations and inventory management. In the wake of improvements in the communication technology, companies are deploying one single ERP system across all factories, offices, departments and locations, thereby ensuring seamless transactions, visibility and controls.

Inventory in the earlier days used to be managed by a system known as cardex system. Bin cards were printed and kept in every bin location. Whenever inventory was put into the bin or removed, the card had to be updated. Apart from the bin cards, books or registers were maintained to note down the transactions and reports were prepared manually. The system was basic and did not provide flexibility to manage warehouse locations as dynamic locations. The operations being manual were time consuming.

In the next phase come the basic inventory management systems, which were a replica of the accounting books containing debit and credit entries along with the balance and the **Cardex System** continued to be used to manage the shop floor operations.

With the **ERP System** introduction, MM modules are deployed which work in tandem with procurement and other modules. Inventory modules contain intelligent applications that manage the inventory, help in analysis, categorization and to a large extent initiate actions and processes based on auto inputs derived from other sources. ERP systems do contain WMS modules, which can be deployed along with the inventory module to manage the warehouse operations. Basic inventory modules in ERP do contain location management of inventory but do not support warehousing operations in detail. **WMS System** applications are designed to work like an extension of the inventory system but are stand alone applications that help in warehousing, control, direct and manage inventory and operations.

In fact a robust system suite comprising of ERP and WMS with interfaces built in between the two systems can play a major role in managing inventory efficiencies.

Both the systems need to be robust, strong and built to suit the business operations requirement as well as logistics operations requirements. While the inventory management efficiencies depend upon the ERP functioning and features, the inventory operations management is heavily dependant upon WMS System.

WMS system is different from an ERP based inventory system in the sense that WMS manages inventory but manages inventory operations and warehouse operations. Though it mirrors the inventory that lies in ERP, the rest of the operations that are carried out through WMS are different and operations intensive. Until a few years ago the inventory operations used to be carried out with basic WMS where most of the operations were manual. Put away lists and pick lists had to be printed and issued to the operators, who had to note down the bin location and the pallet ID etc on the slip and give it back to the operator to do the data entry into the WMS and update the systems. With the introduction of scanning technology things became a lot more easier where barcodes labels could be pasted on the inventory which could then be scanned via hand held or wire less scanners and the data could get uploaded into the WMS. This was further replaced by RF scanners, which work in real time basis.

Today most of the warehouse operations are carried on through RF Scanners, which are like the extension of the WMS and are connected to the system on real time basis. The operators can now download tasks, carry out the tasks and upload confirmation of task completion into the system through RF scanners. This has not only improved operations efficiencies and ensure better house keeping but has greatly improved the inventory as well as data efficiency.

Both ERP and WMS systems along with RF technology have helped improve inventory visibility, accuracy and operations efficiency, resulting in faster operations, leaner inventory and good warehouse management practices.

RF Tag IDs have made an entry into the inventory and supply chain arena and are currently being adapted by retail and textile industries as well as aero spares industry etc. Tag IDs will provide inventory visibility at all times through out the supply chain and thereby ensure inventory accuracy. They are expected to help cut down and ease a lot of operational processes too. However exorbitant cost of the RF tag IDS has been the entry barrier that kept the industries from adapting this technology. The rates are dropping fast making it viable for all industries to adopt these into the inventory management and operations systems.

As compared to the financial accounting, the focus of cost accounting is different. In the modern days of cut throat competition, any business organization has to pay attention towards their cost of production. Computation of cost on scientific basis and thereafter cost control and cost reduction has become of paramount importance. Hence it has become essential to study the basic principles and concepts of cost accounting. These are discussed in the subsequent paragraphs.

Cost :- Cost can be defined as the expenditure (actual or notional) incurred on or attributable to a given thing. It can also be described as the resources that have been sacrificed or must be sacrificed to attain a particular objective. In other words, cost is the amount of resources used for something which must be measured in terms of money. For example – Cost of preparing one cup of tea is the amount incurred on the elements like material, labor and other expenses, similarly cost of offering any services like banking is the amount of expenditure for offering that service. Thus cost of production or cost of service can be calculated by ascertaining the resources used for the production or services.

Costing :-

Costing may be defined as 'the technique and process of ascertaining costs'. According to Wheldon, 'Costing is classifying, recording, allocation and appropriation of expenses for the determination of cost of products or services and for the presentation of suitably arranged data for the purpose of control and guidance of management. It includes the ascertainment of every order, job, contract, process, service units as may be appropriate. It deals with the cost of production, selling and distribution.

If we analyze the above definitions, it will be understood that costing is basically the procedure of ascertaining the costs. As mentioned above, for any business organization, ascertaining of costs is must and for this purpose a scientific procedure should be followed.

'Costing' is precisely this procedure which helps them to find out the costs of products or services.

Cost Accounting :-

Cost Accounting primarily deals with collection, analysis of relevant of cost data for interpretation and presentation for various problems of management. Cost accounting accounts for the cost of products, service or an operation. It is defined as, 'the establishment of budgets, standard costs and actual costs of operations, processes, activities or products and the analysis of variances, profitability or the social use of funds'.

Cost Accountancy :- Cost Accountancy is a broader term and is defined as, 'the application of costing and cost accounting principles, methods and techniques to the science and art and practice of cost control and the ascertainment of profitability as well as presentation of information for the purpose of managerial decision making.' If we analyze the above definition, the following points will emerge,

A. Cost accounting is basically application of the costing and cost accounting principles.

B. This application is with specific purpose and that is for the purpose of cost control, ascertainment of profitability and also for presentation of information to facilitate decision making.

C. Cost accounting is a combination of art and science, it is a science as it has well defined rules and regulations, it is an art as application of any science requires art and it is a practice as it has to be applied on continuous basis and is not a one time exercise.

Objectives of Cost Accounting :- Objectives of Cost Accounting can be summarized as under

1. To ascertain the cost of production on per unit basis, for example, cost per kg, cost per meter, cost per liter, cost per ton etc.

2. Cost accounting helps in the determination of selling price. Cost accounting enables to determine the cost of production on a scientific basis and it helps to fix the selling price.

3. Cost accounting helps in cost control and cost reduction.

4. Ascertainment of division wise, activity wise and unit wise profitability becomes possible through cost accounting.

5. Cost accounting also helps in locating wastages, inefficiencies and other loopholes in the production processes/services offered.

6. Cost accounting helps in presentation of relevant data to the management which helps in decision making. Decision making is one of the important functions of Management and it requires presentation of relevant data. Cost accounting enables presentation of relevant data

in a systematic manner so that decision making becomes possible.

7. Cost accounting also helps in estimation of costs for the future.

Essentials of a good Costing system :-

For availing of maximum benefits, a good costing system should possess the following characteristics.

A. Costing system adopted in any organization should be suitable to its nature and size of the business and its information needs.

B. A costing system should be such that it is economical and the benefits derived from the same should be more than the cost of operating of the same.

C. Costing system should be simple to operate and understand. Unnecessary complications should be avoided.

D. Costing system should ensure proper system of accounting for material, labor and overheads and there should be proper classification made at the time of recording of the transaction itself.

E. Before designing a costing system, need and objectives of the system should be identified.

F. The costing system should ensure that the final aim of ascertaining of cost as accurately possible should be achieved.

Certain Important Terms :- It is necessary to understand certain important terms used in cost accounting.

A. Cost Center :- Cost Center is defined as, 'a production or service, function, activity or item of equipment whose costs may be attributed to cost units. A cost center is the smallest organizational sub unit for which separate cost allocation is attempted'. To put in simple words, a cost center is nothing but a location, person or item of equipment for which cost may be ascertained and used for the purpose of cost control. For example, a production department, stores department, sales department can be cost centers. Similarly, an item of equipment like a lathe, fork-lift, truck or delivery vehicle can be cost center, a person like sales manager can be a cost center. The main object of identifying a cost center is to facilitate collection of costs so that further accounting will be easy. A cost center can be either personal or impersonal, similarly it can be a production cost center or service cost center. A cost center in which a specific process or a continuous sequence of operations is carried out is known as Process Cost Center.

B. Profit Center :- Profit Center is defined as, 'a segment of the business entity by which both revenues are received and expenses are incurred or controlled'. (CEMA) A profit center is any sub unit of an organization to which both revenues and costs are assigned. As explained above, cost center is an activity to which only costs are assigned but a profit center is one where costs and revenues are assigned so that profit can be ascertained. Such revenues and expenditure are being used to evaluate segmental performance as well as managerial performance. A division of an organization may be called as profit center. The performance of profit center is evaluated in terms of the fact whether the center has achieved its budgeted profits. Thus the profit center concept is used for evaluation of performance.

Costing Systems :- There are different costing systems used in practice. These are described below.

A. Historical Costing :- In this system, costs are ascertained only after they are incurred and that is why it is called as historical costing system. For example, costs incurred in the month of April, 2007 may be ascertained and collected in the month of May. Such type of costing system is extremely useful for conducting post-mortem examination of costs, i.e. analysis of the costs incurred in the past. Historical costing system may not be useful from cost control point of view but it certainly indicates a trend in the behavior of costs and is useful for estimation of costs in future.

B. Absorption Costing :- In this type of costing system, costs are absorbed in the product units irrespective of their nature. In other words, all fixed and variable costs are absorbed in the products. It is based on the principle that costs should be charged or absorbed to whatever is being hosted, whether it is a cost unit, cost center.

C. Marginal Costing :- In Marginal Costing, only variable costs are charged to the products and fixed costs are written off to the Costing Profit and Loss A/c. The principle followed in this case is that since fixed costs are largely period costs, they should not enter into the production units. Naturally, the fixed costs will not enter into the inventories and they will be valued at marginal costs only.

D. Uniform Costing :- This is not a distinct method of costing but is the adoption of identical costing principles and procedures by several units of the same industry or by several undertakings by mutual agreement. Uniform costing facilitates valid comparisons between organizations and helps in eliminating inefficiencies.

Classification of Costs :-

An important step in computation and analysis of cost is the classification of costs into different types. Classification helps in better control of the costs and also helps considerably in decision making. Classification of costs can be made according to the following basis.

A. Classification according to elements :- Costs can be classified according to the elements. There are three elements of costing, viz. material, labor and expenses. Total cost of production/ services can be divided into the three elements to find out the contribution of each element in the total costs.

B. Classification according to nature :- As per this classification, costs can be classified into Direct and Indirect. Direct costs are the costs which are identifiable with the product unit or cost center while indirect costs are not identifiable with the product unit or cost center and hence they are to be allocated, apportioned and then absorb in the production units. All elements of costs like material, labor and expenses can be classified into direct and indirect. They are mentioned below.

i. Direct and Indirect Material :- Direct material is the material which is identifiable with the product. For example, in a cup of tea, quantity of milk consumed can be identified, quantity of glass in a glass bottle can be identified and so these will be direct materials

for these products. Indirect material cannot be identified with the product, for example lubricants, fuel, oil, cotton wastes etc cannot be identified with a given unit of product and hence these are the examples of indirect materials.

ii. Direct and Indirect Labor :- Direct labor can be identified with a given unit of product, for example, when wages are paid according to the piece rate, wages per unit can be identified. Similarly wages paid to workers who are directly engaged in the production can also be identified and hence they are direct wages. On the other hand, wages paid to workers like sweepers, gardeners, maintenance workers etc are indirect wages as they cannot be identified with the given unit of production.

iii. Direct and Indirect Expenses :- Direct expenses refers to expenses that are specifically incurred and charged for specific or particular job, process, service, cost center or cost unit. These expenses are also called as chargeable expenses. Examples of these expenses are cost of drawing, design and layout, royalties payable on use of patents, copyrights etc, consultation fees paid to architects, surveyors etc. Indirect expenses on the other hand cannot be traced to specific product, job, process, service or cost center or cost unit. Several examples of indirect expenses can be given like insurance, electricity, rent, salaries, advertising etc. It should be noted that the total of direct expenses is known as 'Prime Cost' while the total of all indirect expenses is known as 'Overheads'.

C. Classification according to behavior :- Costs can also be classified according to their behavior.

This classification is explained below.

i. Fixed Costs :- Out of the total costs, some costs remain fixed irrespective of changes in the production volume. These costs are called as fixed costs. The feature of these costs is that the total costs remain same while per unit fixed cost is always variable. Examples of these costs are salaries, insurance, rent, etc.

ii. Variable Costs :- These costs are variable in nature, i.e. they change according to the volume of production. Their variability is in the same proportion to the production. For example, if the production units are 2,000 and the variable cost is Rs. 5 per unit, the total variable cost will be Rs. 10,000, if the production units are increased to 5,000 units, the total variable costs will be Rs. 25,000, i.e. the increase is exactly in the same proportion of the production. Another feature of the variable cost is that per unit variable cost remains same while the total variable costs will vary. In the example given above, the per unit variable cost remains Rs. 2 per unit while total variable costs change. Examples of variable costs are direct materials, direct labor etc.

iii. Semi-variable Costs :- Certain costs are partly fixed and partly variable. In other words, they contain the features of both types of costs. These costs are neither totally fixed nor totally variable. Maintenance costs, supervisory costs etc are examples of semi-variable costs. These costs are also called as 'stepped costs'.

D. Classification according to functions :- Costs can also be classified according to the functions/ activities. This classification can be done as mentioned below.

i. Production Costs :- All costs incurred for production of goods are known as production costs.

ii. Administrative Costs :- Costs incurred for administration are known as administrative costs. Examples of these costs are office salaries, printing and stationery, office telephone, office rent, office insurance etc.

iii. Selling and Distribution Costs :- All costs incurred for procuring an order are called as selling costs while all costs incurred for execution of order are distribution costs. Market research expenses, advertising, sales staff salary, sales promotion expenses are some of the examples of selling costs. Transportation expenses incurred on sales, warehouse rent etc are examples of distribution costs.

iv. Research and Development Costs :- In the modern days, research and development has become one of the important functions of a business organization.

Expenditure incurred for this function can be classified as Research and Development Costs.

E. Classification according to time :- Costs can also be classified according to time. This classification is explained below.

I. Historical Costs :- These are the costs which are incurred in the past, i.e. in the past year, past month or even in the last week or yesterday. The historical costs are ascertained after the period is over. In other words it becomes a post-mortem analysis of what has happened in the past. Though historical costs have limited importance, still they can be used for estimating the trends of the future, i.e. they can be effectively used for predicting the future costs.

II. Predetermined Cost :- These costs relating to the product are computed in advance of production, on the basis of a specification of all the factors affecting cost and cost data. Pre determined costs may be either standard or estimated. Standard Cost is a predetermined calculation of how much cost should be under specific working conditions. It is based on technical studies regarding material, labor and expenses. The main purpose of standard cost is to have some kind of benchmark for comparing the actual performance with the standards. On the other hand, estimated costs are predetermined costs based on past performance and adjusted to the anticipated changes. It can be used in any business situation or decision making which does not require accurate cost.

F. Classification of costs for Management decision making :- One of the important function of cost accounting is to present information to the Management for the purpose of decision making. For decision making certain types of costs are relevant. Classification of costs based on the criteria of decision making can be done in the following manner

I. Marginal Cost :- Marginal cost is the change in the aggregate costs due to change in the volume of output by one unit. For example, suppose a manufacturing company produces 10,000 units and the aggregate costs are Rs. 25,000, if 10,001 units are produced the aggregate costs may be Rs. 25,020 which means that the marginal cost is Rs. 20. Marginal cost is also termed as variable cost and hence per unit marginal cost is always same, i.e. per unit marginal cost is always fixed. Marginal cost can be effectively used for decision making in various areas.

II. Differential Costs :- Differential costs are also known as incremental cost. This cost is the difference in total cost that will arise from the selection of one alternative to the other. In other words, it is an added cost of a change in the level of activity. This type of analysis is useful for taking various decisions like change in the level of activity, adding or dropping a product, change in product mix, make or buy decisions, accepting an export offer and so on.

III. Opportunity Costs :- It is the value of benefit sacrificed in favor of an alternative course of action. It is the maximum amount that could be obtained at any given point of time if a resource was sold or put to the most valuable alternative use that would be practicable. Opportunity cost of goods or services is measured in terms of revenue which could have been earned by employing that goods or services in some other alternative uses.

IV. Relevant Cost :- The relevant cost is a cost which is relevant in various decisions of management. Decision making involves consideration of several alternative courses of action. In this process, whatever costs are relevant are to be taken into consideration. In other words, costs which are going to be affected matter the most and these costs are called as relevant costs. Relevant cost is a future cost which is different for different alternatives. It can also be defined as any cost which is affected by the decision on hand. Thus in decision making relevant costs play a vital role.

V. Replacement Cost :- This cost is the cost at which existing items of material or fixed assets can be replaced. Thus this is the cost of replacing existing assets at present or at a future date.

VI. Abnormal Costs :- It is an unusual or a typical cost whose occurrence is usually not regular and is unexpected. This cost arises due to some abnormal situation of production. Abnormal cost arises due to idle time, may be due to some unexpected heavy breakdown of machinery.

They are not taken into consideration while computing cost of production or for decision making.

VII. Controllable Costs :- In cost accounting, cost control and cost reduction are extremely important. In fact, in the competitive environment, cost control and reduction are the key words. Hence it is essential to identify the controllable and uncontrollable costs.

Controllable costs are those which can be controlled or influenced by a conscious management action. For example, costs like telephone, printing stationery etc can be controlled while costs like salaries etc cannot be controlled at least in the short run. Generally, direct costs are controllable while uncontrollable costs are beyond the control of an individual in a given period of time.

VIII. Shutdown Cost :- These costs are the costs which are incurred if the operations are shut down and they will disappear if the operations are continued. Examples of these costs are costs of sheltering the plant and machinery and construction of sheds for storing exposed property. Computation of shutdown costs is extremely important for taking a decision of continuing or shutting down operations.

IX. Capacity Cost :- These costs are normally fixed costs. The cost incurred by a company for providing production, administration and selling and distribution capabilities in order to perform various functions. Capacity costs include the costs of plant, machinery and building for production, warehouses and vehicles for distribution and key personnel for administration. These costs are in the nature of long-term costs and are incurred as a result of planning decisions.

X. Urgent Costs :- These costs are those which must be incurred in order to continue operations of the firm. For example, cost of material and labor must be incurred if production is to take place.

Costing Methods and Techniques :-

Introduction :- It is necessary to understand the difference between the costing methods and techniques. Costing methods are those which help a firm to compute the cost of production or services offered by it. On the other hand, costing techniques are those which help a firm to present the data in a particular manner so as to facilitate the decision making as well as cost control and cost reduction. Costing methods and techniques are explained below.

Methods of Costing :- The following are the methods of costing.

I. Job Costing :- This method is also called as job costing. This costing method is used in firms which work on the basis of job work. There are some manufacturing units which undertake job work and are called as job order units. The main feature of these organizations is that they produce according to the requirements and specifications of the consumers. Each job may be different from the other one. Production is only on specific order and there is no pre demand production. Because of this situation, it is necessary to compute the cost of each job and hence job costing system is used. In this system, each job is treated separately and a job cost sheet is prepared to find out the cost of the job. The job cost sheet helps to compute the cost of the job in a phased manner and finally arrives the total cost of production.

II. Batch Costing :- This method of costing is used in those firms where production is made on continuous basis. Each unit coming out is uniform in all respects and production is made prior to the demand, i.e. in anticipation of demand. One batch of production consists of the units produced from the time machinery is set to the time when it will be shut down for maintenance. For example, if production commences on 1st January 2007 and the machine is shut down for maintenance on 1st April 2007, the number of units produced in this period will be the size of one batch. The total cost incurred during this period will be divided by the number of units produced and unit cost will be worked out. Firms producing consumer goods like television, air-conditioners, washing machines etc use batch costing.

III. Process Costing :- Some of the products like sugar, chemicals etc involve continuous production process and hence process costing method is used to work out the cost of production. The meaning of continuous process is that the input introduced in the process I travels through continuous process before finished product is produced.

The output of process I becomes input of process II and the output of process II becomes input of the process III. If there is no additional process, the output of process III will be the finished product. In process costing, cost per process is worked out and per unit cost is worked out by dividing the total cost by the number of units. Industries like sugar, edible oil, chemicals are examples of continuous production process and use process costing.

IV. Operating Costing :- This type of costing method is used in service sector to work out the cost of services offered to the consumers. For example, operating costing method is used in hospitals, power generating units, transportation sector etc. A cost sheet is prepared to compute the total cost and it is divided by cost units for working out the per unit cost.

V. Contract Costing :- This method of costing is used in construction industry to work out the cost of contract undertaken. For example, cost of constructing a bridge, commercial complex, residential complex, highways etc is worked out by use of this method of costing. Contract costing is actually similar to job costing, the only difference being that in contract costing, one construction job may take several months or even years before they are complete while in job costing, each job may be of a short duration. In contract costing, as each contract may take a long period for completion, the question of computing of profit is to be solved with the help of a well defined and accepted method.

Technique of Costing :- As mentioned above, costing methods are for computation of the total cost of production/services offered by a firm. On the other hand, costing technique help to present the data in a particular format so that decision making becomes easy. Costing techniques also help for controlling and reducing the costs. The following are the techniques of costing.

I. Marginal Costing :- This technique is based on the assumption that the total cost of production can be divided into fixed and variable. Fixed costs remain same irrespective of the changes in the volume of production while the variable costs vary with the level of production, i.e. they will increase if the production increases and decrease if the production decreases. Variable cost per unit always remains the same. In this technique, only variable costs are taken into account while calculating production cost. Fixed costs are not absorbed in the production units. They are written off to the Costing Profit and Loss Account. The reason behind this is that the fixed costs are period costs and hence should not be absorbed in the production. Secondly they are variable on per unit basis and hence there is no equitable basis for charging

them to the products. This technique is effectively used for decision making in the areas like make or buy decisions, optimizing of product mix, key factor analysis, fixation of selling price, accepting or rejecting an export offer, and several other areas.

II. Standard Costing :- Standard costs are predetermined costs relating to material, labor and overheads. Though they are predetermined, they are worked out on scientific basis by conducting technical analysis. They are computed for all elements of costs such as material, labor and overheads. The main objective of fixation of standard cost is to have benchmark against which the actual performance can be compared. This means that the actual costs are compared with the standards. The difference is called as 'variance'. If actual costs are more than the standard, the variance is 'adverse' while if actual costs are less than the standard, the variance is 'favorable'. The adverse variances are analyzed and reasons for the same are found out. Favorable variances may also be analyzed to find out the reasons behind the same. Standard costing, thus is an important technique for cost control and reduction.

III. Budgets and Budgetary Control :- Budget is defined as, 'a quantitative and/or a monetary statement prepared to prior to a defined period of time for the policies during that period for the purpose of achieving a given objective.' If we analyze this definition, it will be clear that a budget is a statement, which may be either in monetary form or quantitative form or both. For example, a production budget can be prepared in quantitative form showing the target production, it can also be prepared in monetary terms showing the expected cost of production. Some budgets can be prepared only in monetary terms, e.g. cash budget showing the estimated receipts and payments in a particular period can be prepared in monetary terms only.

Another feature of budget is that it is always prepared prior to a defined period of time which means that budget is always prepared for future and that too a defined future. For example, a budget may be prepared for next 12 months or 6 months or even for 1 month, but the time period must be certain and not vague. One of the important aspect of budgeting is that it lays down the objective to be achieved during the defined period of time and for achieving the objectives, whatever policies are to be pursued are reflected in the budget. Budgetary control involves preparation of budgets and continuous comparison of actual with budgets so that necessary corrective action can be taken. For example, when a production budget is prepared, the production targets are laid down in the same for a particular period.

After the period is over, the actual production is compared with the budget and the deviation is found out so that necessary corrective action can be taken. Budget and Budgetary Control is one of the important techniques of costing used for cost control and also for performance evaluation. The success of the technique depends upon several factors such as support from top management, involvement of employees and coordination within the organization.